THE GOD OF ELIJAH

By
Dr D. K. Olukoya

THE GOD OF ELIJAH
© 2010 DR. D. K. OLUKOYA
ISBN: 978 - 978 - 49174 - 7 - 6

Printed and published in Nigeria ©2010 by :
Mountain of Fire and Miracles Ministries
13, Olasimbo street, off Olumo road,
(by UNILAG second gate)
Onike, Iwaya. Lagos.

For further information or permission, contact:
Email: pasteurdanielolukoya_french@yahoo.fr
mfmhqworldwide@mountainoffire.org

Or visit our website: www.mountainoffire.org

Introduction

Beloved, the intent and purpose of our message is to appreciate our Lord God from the view point of that great prophet, Elijah. You will recall that it is written that Elijah was a man of like passion as you and I, yet our Lord God manifested Himself in his life in such extraordinary ways that sometimes makes one wonder why such responses from God·are not so common today. What was it about Elijah that distinguished him from the rest and made God so endeared to him? This is what this book is all about.

Where is the Lord God of Elijah?

Our first scripture is taken from 2 Kings 2:11-14,

"And it came to pass as they still went on and talked that behold, there appeared a chariot of fire and horses of fire and parted them both asunder and Elijah went up by a whirlwind into heaven: And Elisha saw it, and he cried, My father, my father, the chariot of Israel and the horsemen thereof: And he saw him no more: and he took hold of his own clothes, and rent them in two pieces. He took up also the mantle of Elijah that fell from him and went back, and stood by the bank of Jordan. And he took the mantle of Elijah that fell from him and smote the waters and said. "Where is the Lord God of Elijah?" And when he also had smitten the waters, they parted hither and thither and Elisha went over."

There is a significant position for Elijah in the whole of God's programme. Look at Malachi 4:5-6

"Behold, I will send you Elijah the Prophet before the coming of the great and dreadful day of the Lord. And he shall turn the heart of the fathers to the children and the heart of the children to their fathers, lest I come and smite the earth with a curse."

So, if Elijah did not come, the Lord said He will smite the earth with a curse. Luke I: 5-30 tells us the wonderful story of John the Baptist; the way he was conceived and the prophecy about him. For 400 years, God did not speak to anybody and the first time He decided to start talking was through a tremendous and wonderful man called John the Baptist, a fore-runner of the Lord Jesus Christ. The Bible says that "There is no prophet greater than him." How can a prophet be greater than a fore runner of the Lord Jesus Christ? It is not possible. Jesus Christ is the fullness of the divine revelation to man. So anybody that came to advertise Him has to be the greatest of the prophets. Luke 1:12-13 says,

"And when Zacharias saw him, he was troubled and fear fell upon him. But the angel said unto him. Fear not, Zacharias: for thy prayer is heard; and thy wife Elizabeth shall bear thee a son, and thou shalt call his name John."

Then in verse 14, He gave a wonderful prophecy;

"Thou shall have joy and gladness: and many shall rejoice at his birth. For he shall be great in the sight of the Lord and shall drink neither wine nor strong drink, and he shall be filled with the Holy Ghost even from his mother's womb. And many of the children of Israel shall turn to the Lord their God. And he shall go before him in the spirit and power of Elias, to turn the hearts of the fathers to the children and the disobedient to the wisdom of the just; to

make ready a people prepared for the Lord."

When John the Baptist was born, he was an unusual man. If Elijah and John the Baptist were to be pastors of churches today, I am sure many people will run away from them, because fire will fall down on fornicators inside the service, and they will roast there or sinners would be somersaulting at the back for committing an offence against the Lord God of Elijah.

In addition their clothes would smell, because they did not change clothes too often neither did they put on perfume, but they had power. Please note, we do not say that people should not have their baths. No, after all, physical cleanliness is said to be a good compliment of godliness. One good thing about the ministry of John the Baptist is that he was a very precise person. He always went straight to the point and his words were like fire. It was John the Baptist that said, "*The axe is laid to the root of every tree and any tree that does not bear a good fruit shall be cut down and thrown into fire*." Luke 3:9. He was the one that called the scribes and Pharisees. *"You generation of vipers, who asked you to flee from the wrath to come?"* Matthew 3:7. Hot messages! Those are the kinds of preachers we need now. The Elijah kind of message, the Elijah kind of spirit, the Elijah kind of power; the spirit of violence in the kingdom. Those are the kinds of people we need to operate in our generation. The church of God is not looking for cosmetologists or powerful dressers, what we need in the house of God now, are surgeons who would take knife and cut her through. It may be painful but these are the kind of pastors that we need now whose messages are the messages of the last days. The message of John the Baptist was "*Any tree that does not bear good fruit shall be* cut down and thrown into the fire." And God is still doing that now. All the useless trees growing in the house of God, all the useless ministers, useless workers, useless members, that are all over the places are now being cut down and removed as the last days are here. Where do you stand? That is the question.

When Jesus was leaving the earth, his disciples did not know the kind of kingdom that Jesus came for. They asked foolish and political questions like, "O Lord, will you at this time restore the kingdom to Israel?" It was painful to Jesus. They were all looking for different things just as there were many people at the cross who only came to spectate. Even when Jesus was on earth, they were looking for the wrong things. Somebody like the thief, Judas Iscariot also would have said, "When will this man take over the government and make somebody like me a governor, so that I can steal *money.*" Judas knew that Jesus had power to take over because several times they wanted to make Jesus king but he ran away. Judas knew that he had that power to rule if he so desired. But Jesus was not interested in ruling, so when he saw that his desires and ambitions were failing, he went and betrayed him. His inordinate ambitions had blinded him from seeing the real blessings that Jesus came for.

The other disciples too like John and his brother were more occupied with sitting at the right hand and at the left hand of God, in the kingdom of Heaven when they were still living here on earth. They wanted promotion without work; their cares were more in their personal glory. People like Thomas, as an academic man rationalised everything; he could not even believe the words of his own master as to his return. Someone like Peter did not want Jesus to die for ever: They were all selfish. There are some people in the church who work hard only when they see the General Overseer. That is "Eye service." It shows they are not serious. I hope you are not like that; "Show-glass Christians."

Jesus told them that it was not for you to know the time and season, the Father Almighty has fixed by His authority to return the kingdom to Israel. Jesus said it was not for them to know but that they shall receive power after the Holy Ghost has come upon them, and they shall be His witnesses in Jerusalem, Judea, Samaria and unto the utter most part of the earth. After the Pentecost, they did not preach the kind of message Jesus wanted them to preach in Jerusalem. The only man that preached the correct message of the spirit and power like Elijah was one man called Stephen. By the time he finished, people were grinding their teeth. The Bible says, they put their fingers in their ears; they did not want to hear anymore of what Stephen had to say and they pounced on him at the same time at the command of the devil.

Unfortunately beloved, what many of us want is not what we need. The Bible says, the time is coming when they shall no longer listen to sound doctrine, but they shall look for their own preachers who will be tickling their ears and be exciting them; a sinner is jumping up on one leg and shouting on stage and preaching cute messages and people just love him for that. A satanic deception and error of the last days. It is that message we need now and it is with the same spirit and power that we can operate in the last days. Elijah operated at a time when the powers of darkness had completely paralyzed Israel so much that they threw down the altars of God and forgot about serving God. So, when Elijah ended up at the celebrated contest at Mount Camel, the first thing he did was to repair the altar of God that had been broken down. They had forgotten the worship of Yahweh and were worshiping. Baal. That was the level Israel got to and Ahab was in-charge. Ahab was a female-man controlled by his demonic wife, Jezebel who brought the demon from her country and established it in the whole place. That was the time Elijah came. We need that kind of ministry now; the ministry of fire and power and for us to have it, we must work harder than we are doing now. If you have spent a year or two in MFM and you can still sit down and say, "I do not know why this person is making face at me," God have mercy on you. For how long will you tarry in the primary school department of faith? When will you grow above malice, envy, playing with your enemies and leaving your target to fight shadows? Think about it. We are supposed to move in that kind of ministry. Our shadows are supposed to chase demons. That is how the God of Elijah operates. When we are passing by, witches and wizards are supposed to be hiding from us. Our houses should be so charged that it is only a witch that wants to commit suicide that will decide to fly over them. Even the saliva from our mouths should become fire and if you spit the saliva on the floor and somebody decides to collect the sand and use it for evil purpose, it would explode in his hands. This is how God wants us to move.

I remember the church I was with many years ago. Everybody knew that anytime we gathered for service, we were at the war front. I find it difficult to believe today, how a serious man of God can wear a whole 10 yards of clothes (agbada) that makes it difficult for him to move and he is busy folding it up and down when there is a lot of work to do. In that church, if you wore agbada (African design) there, you would carry a demon home. If you want to survive in that kind of place, you have to be on fire just like any man of God that wants to survive now. The issue of fornication and adultery are supposed to have disappeared from your life as a believer. But if you are still battling with these, you cannot be in the last day army. In that place, when we start praying, unbelievers became afraid of taking the bridge by the back of our church. Only born again Christians could use the bridge. Some of them even started speaking in tongues without being our members.

Instead of evil people running from one herbalist to the other looking for how to deal with a Christian, the reverse is the case. It is Christians that are running around seeking for counselling against evil spirits. Your lot as a believer is that if somebody takes your case to herbalists, they will refuse to work with your name. Why is it that many of us have never even seen one single angel in our dream, let alone recognising them physically? Whereas in those days when they lock people up, angels come to set them free. Why? It is because we are not consecrated enough. We have been wrongly programmed.

What do we do?

We need to call on the God of Elijah. And when we call upon Him, things will begin to happen. Many of us need to be touched a second time. That you have been speaking in tongues for five years will not help you. You need to collect a new fire. Let fresh fire of the Almighty start to burn in your life. Drop the primary school things. The Bible says some people when they are supposed to be adults, are still babies. At such time they are supposed to be teachers, they themselves need to be taught the basics of the doctrine of Christ. There are some of us who used to be healthy before, but now they are sick. Such people still carry tablets in their bags when they come to spiritual clinics. Some used to see visions of heaven and the Lord Jesus but now it is bad dreams or slender beautiful women. Believers who are meant to vomit fire on the enemies are eating in their dreams and seeing the dead. Some used to hear music from heaven; but now they are hearing strange noises. God used to speak to some people clearly before but now they hear very little. We need to call on the God of Elijah.

Elijah was an important prophet in the Old and New Testament. Although we do not know much about his parents, yet he made history in the name of the Lord. He was the first prophet to announce that there will be drought to punish God's enemies. He was the first prophet to lock up heaven and put the key in his pocket and said, "There will be no rain except by my word;" the first prophet to multiply food, raise the dead, pray for immediate rain, write a death letter to a king and the first prophet to call down fire. When Elijah had gone by a whirlwind to heaven, his servant was stuck at a place called "Jordan." He could not build a bridge to pass nor swim over. He was in trouble and could not do anything. He would have been destroyed by wild animals but then he screamed, *"Where is the Lord God of Elijah?"* And as he did that, that God answered.

Who then is the Lord God of Elijah?

1. The Lord God of Elijah is the one that makes a way where there is no way. He can path your Jordan so that you can cross over.
2. The God that multiplies with nothing.
3. The God that brings the visible out of the invisible.
4. The God that can provide for His people by humanly impossible means. The Lord God of Elijah was the one that fed Elijah through the ravens.
5. He is the one who looks after all those who loose themselves in Him, like the widow of Zarephat.
6. He is the God of resurrection. He gave power unto dead bones, and they came alive again.
7. He is the Lord that can give supernatural strength. Elijah ran 30 miles by feet and the chariots could not catch up with him.

The Lord of supernatural energy.
8. The Lord God of Elijah is the God that answereth by fire.

May be you are at the end of the road now and a particular problem seems to have caged you in, call on the Lord God of Elijah, let Him answer by fire. One big truth is that the man who can really pray has nothing to fear. Lots of people are at the point of despair and the Bible does not want anybody to despair. Sometime ago, a sister was planning to move out of her husband's house because they were barely able to eat half a meal a day. Her salary and that of her husband put together would not even pay the house rent let alone buy food. The husband was praying for breakthrough. One day, in anger, he called on the God of Elijah to answer by fire before going to work. He could speak Arabic and English languages. His work was to serve food in a

Restaurant.

One day, an Arab came to eat in the Restaurant and could not place his orders because he could not speak English. So, this brother helped him out. And the man was happy to meet somebody who could speak Arabic. As he was eating, he called this brother and wanted to give him another job after asking for his salary. The Arab man offered him a job as his interpreter with a salary of 1,000 pounds a day. The brother thought he was joking. The Arab paid him a month in advance and so the brother resigned and they left together. When the brother got home and showed madam the money; madam ran mad. She could not believe him for ten minutes.

That is what happens when a person decides to call upon the God of Elijah. He will always answer by fire. You are going to call on the Lord God of Elijah like Elisha did when he was by his own River Jordan.

You might have arrived at your own River Jordan and enemies are laughing at you and asking you to show them what your God can do. It is also good to tell them, "I serve the God that answereth by Fire."

PRAYER POINTS

1. I will not reap any satanic harvest, in the name of Jesus.

2. Untouchable power, indestructible power and unchallengeable power fall upon my life now, in the name of Jesus.

3. Let the fire of the Almighty God soak my hands now, in the name of Jesus.

4. Let fire come down and suppress all my oppressors, in the name of Jesus.

5. Let the God of Elijah divide my Jordan, in the name of Jesus.

6. Lord God of Elijah, convert my disappointments to miracles, in the name of Jesus.

7. Lord God of Elijah, sack all those who are sitting on my seat, in the name of Jesus.

8. Lord God of Elijah, bring the visible out of the invisible for me, in the name of Jesus.

   Sing "The God that answereth by fire, He will be my God."

9. Lord God of Elijah, paralyse every household wickedness in the name of Jesus.

   Sing, "Let there be glory, and honour and praises, glory and honour to Jesus, let there be glory, let there be honour, glory and honour to Him."

10. Lord God of Elijah, remove inherited limitations from my life, in Jesus' name.

About the author

Dr. D. K. Olukoya

Dr. Daniel Kolawole Olukoya, by the grace of God, is the founder and General Overseer of Mountain of Fire and Miracles Ministries (Worldwide), and The Battle Cry Christian Ministries, (Worldwide).

Dr. Olukoya holds a first class honours degree in Microbiology from the University of Lagos, Nigeria and a PhD in Molecular Genetics from the University of Reading, United Kingdom.

As a researcher, he has over **70 scientific publications** to his credit.

Anointed by God, Dr. Olukoya is a prophet, evangelist, teacher and preacher of the word. His life and that of his wife, Shade, and their son, Elijah Toluwani, are living proofs that all power belongs to God.

He has over **100 Christian publications.**

Made in the USA
Lexington, KY
10 June 2015